The Fall of Ken Paxton: Texas's Republican Attorney General Faces Impeachment

By

Gregory D. Richardson

Copyright

Table of Content

Chapter 1: Why Texas' GOP-controlled House Wants to Impeach Republican Attorney General Ken Paxton

The Republican-controlled Texas House of Representatives is moving toward an impeachment vote on Saturday that could rapidly remove Republican Attorney General Ken Paxton from office after years of legal and ethical issues involving him.

In the closing days of the state's legislative session, an exceptional and hardly employed tactic sets up a brutal political conflict. It puts House Republican leadership, who now seems to have had enough of the accusations of impropriety that have long followed

Texas' top attorney, against Paxton, who has allied himself firmly with former President Donald Trump and the state's hard-right conservatives.

Paxton is opposing it at every turn, branding the whole process "corrupt." During the voting, he urged his fans to gather in his support at the state Capitol.

Following is an explanation of Texas's impeachment procedure and how the 60-year-old Republican came to be faced with the possibility of being the state's third official to be impeached in its almost 200-year history:

THE PROCEEDING

According to Texas law and the state constitution, the procedure for impeaching a state official begins in the state House, just as it does for federal officials.

The 149-member House General Investigating Committee unanimously agreed to submit 20 articles of impeachment in this matter on Thursday. The committee's five members.

Paxton must do bleak legislative math. To impeach, just a simple majority is required. That indicates that if all 64 Democrats vote against Trump, just a tiny portion of the

House's 85 Republicans would need to do the same.

However, the investigative committee has testified before recommending impeachment, thus the House is not required to do so. Investigators gave Paxton's years-long controversy and suspected law-breaking an unusual public airing over many hours on Wednesday.

The floor discussion and vote on Saturday are anticipated to run almost five hours.

If the House impeaches Paxton, the Senate will determine whether to convict him or permanently remove him from office. A majority vote of two-thirds is necessary for removal by the Senate.

A SUSPECTED PERIL

But there is a significant distinction between the Texas system and the federal one: If Paxton is found guilty, he is immediately removed from office until the verdict of the Senate trial. The temporary successor would be chosen by Republican Governor Greg Abbott.

In Texas, the GOP is in charge of all state government institutions. Up until this week, Republican legislators and leaders maintained a low profile on the many instances of Paxton's alleged misbehavior and violation of the law that have come to light in court documents and press stories over the years.

Paxton settled a whistleblower case in February that was filed by former aides who had accused him of wrongdoing. The House must approve the $3.3 million compensation, but Republican Speaker Dade Phelan has said he does not believe taxpayers should bear the cost.

The House probe against Paxton started soon after the settlement was finalized.

The investigation committee said in a letter on Friday that Paxton would not be facing impeachment "but for his request for a taxpayer-funded settlement over his wrongful conduct."

THE SETTING

Paxton has urged supporters from around the state to congregate at the Capitol and have a peaceful protest while the vote is taking place inside the House chamber.

Use your government's petitioning process. Let's give the people of this wonderful state their authority back, not the politicians," Paxton added.

The proposal was similar to one made by Trump on January 6, 2021, when a crowd forcefully stormed the U.S. Capitol in Washington, DC, to protest his presidential failure. Before the uprising, Paxton spoke at a rally in Washington.

Gov. Abbott, who has been silent on the impeachment process, will address members in the House chamber on Memorial Day a few hours before the vote.

Recent weeks have seen raucous protests about gun and LGBTQ+ rights bills at the Capitol and in the House gallery. After demonstrations against a bill to outlaw transgender medical treatment for kids broke out, hundreds of state police officers had to evacuate the gallery and Capitol rotunda.

REPUBLICAN AGAINST REPUBLICAN

Contrary to the most notable recent precedents of impeachment in America, the five-member committee that conducted the inquiry on Paxton is run by his fellow Republicans.

Democrats who had a majority in the U.S. House of Representatives were the driving force behind Trump's federal impeachments in 2020 and 2021. Both times, the Senate rejected the House-approved impeachment accusations because Republicans had the necessary number of votes to prevent conviction.

Republicans possess a resounding majority in both houses of the legislature in Texas, and they also occupy all of the state's influential positions. Even yet, Paxton continues to make efforts to organize a partisan defense.

Tuesday, when news of the House probe broke, Paxton said Phelan had launched a political assault. During a lengthy session last Friday, he demanded the "liberal" speaker's resignation and said that he had been intoxicated.

The charge was dismissed by Phelan's office as Paxton trying to "save face."

Since then, none of the other leading Republicans in the state who were elected have endorsed Paxton. However, the state party's head defended him on Friday, labeling the impeachment attempt a "sham" based on "allegations already litigated by voters."

Matt Rinaldi, chairman of the Republican Party, said that they will depend on the "principled leadership of the Texas Senate to restore sanity and reason."

On Thursday, Paxton also claimed that the impeachment process was an attempt to deny voting rights to those who had supported him in his November election for a third term. As a result of their opposition to him, he said, "The RINOs in the Texas Legislature are now on the same side as Joe Biden."

THE WEAKNESS IN MARRIAGE

But Paxton, who was attorney general after serving five years in the House and one in the Senate, is certain to still have friends in Austin.

One is his wife Angela, a two-term state senator who could find herself in the uncomfortable position of casting a vote that would determine her husband's political destiny. She may or might not take part in the Senate trial, where the 31 senators make the margins narrow.

In an unexpected turn of events, Paxton's impeachment involves an extramarital affair he confessed to staff members years previously. The impeachment allegations include bribery for Nate Paul, an Austin real estate developer who is one of Paxton's contributors and is accused of hiring the lady with whom he had an affair in return for legal assistance.

YEARS OF PREPARATION

The accusations of securities fraud for which Paxton was charged in 2015 and hasn't yet been tried are the basis for the impeachment. Paxton was accused by the legislators of lying to state securities authorities.

However, Paxton's links to Paul and a noteworthy uprising by the attorney general's senior assistants in 2020 are the main sources of the stories.

Eight top Paxton aides accused their boss of bribes and using his position improperly to boost Paul that autumn, and they denounced him to the FBI. Later, four of them filed the whistleblower complaint. The story sparked a federal criminal investigation, which in February was taken over by the Public Integrity Section of the U.S. Justice Department in Washington.

There are several allegations about Paxton's interactions with Paul included in the impeachment charges. Allegations include attempting to sabotage foreclosure litigation, unlawfully providing Paul with legal advice, and terminating, intimidating, and interfering with personnel who brought up the issue. The alleged bribery occurred as a result of the romance and Paul's alleged payment for Paxton's Austin home's pricey improvements.

The conflict hurt the Texas attorney general's office, which had long been one of the main legal foes of Democratic White House administrations.

Since Paxton's team joined the FBI, his organization has been in chaos on the inside, with seasoned attorneys leaving over tactics they claim are intended to skew legal work, reward devoted employees, and silence dissenters.

HISTORY OF TEXAS

For his unusual plea that the U.S. Supreme Court invalidates Biden's victory over Trump in the 2020 presidential election, Paxton was already going to make history. He may now change the course of history.

The Texas House has only twice removed a sitting official from office.

James "Pa" Ferguson, the governor, was ousted from office in 1917 due to misuse of public finances, theft, and the diverting of a special fund. O.P. Carrillo, a state judge, was removed from office in 1975 for submitting fake financial statements and diverting equipment and funds from the government for personal use.

Chapter 2: Paxton Invites Supporters to Rally to Protest the Impeachment Vote.

When Republicans in the House of Representatives take up unprecedented impeachment procedures that threaten to remove him, Texas Attorney General Ken Paxton on Friday asked his supporters to demonstrate in the state Capitol.

The House has scheduled a vote for this coming Saturday to decide whether to convict Paxton of bribery, declare him ineligible for office, or remove him from office altogether. These are just a few of the charges that have dogged Paxton for most of his three tenure.

Republican Paxton, 60, criticized the impeachment process as "political theater" that would "inflict lasting damage on the Texas House," adding to his prior assertions that it is an attempt to deny the people who elected him in November their right to vote.

At a press conference, he said, "I want to invite my fellow citizens and friends to peacefully come let their voices be heard at the Capitol tomorrow." He did not take any questions. Use your legal authority to write to your government.

This proposal is reminiscent of the one made by former President Donald Trump on January 6, 2021, when a crowd brutally stormed the U.S. Capitol in Washington,

DC, to protest his election loss. Paxton, who spoke at the rally that preceded that uprising, summoned his supporters to the Texas Capitol on the day the governor was scheduled to address legislators in observance of Memorial Day.

If Paxton were to be impeached, the Republican governor Greg Abbott could select a temporary successor while Paxton was immediately suspended from duty. The attorney general would be the first statewide official since former governor James "Pa" Ferguson in 1917 and only the third person in the state's almost 200-year history to be impeached.

According to a statement issued Friday by the House Committee on General

Investigating, the House will start debating a resolution demanding Paxton's impeachment at 1 p.m. Saturday.

Paxton was the subject of a covert investigation by a GOP-led committee that recommended his impeachment on Thursday based on 20 articles. According to Paxton, the accusations are supported by "hearsay and rumors, repeating long-disproven claims."

Famous conservatives had been unusually silent on Paxton, but several started to support him on Friday. Matt Rinaldi, the head of the state Republican Party, called the trial a "sham" and encouraged the Republican-controlled Senate to acquit Paxton if he were to be tried there.

Rinaldi echoed Paxton's criticism of Republican House Speaker Dade Phelan, saying, "It is based on allegations already litigated by voters, led by a liberal speaker trying to undermine his conservative adversaries." The Senate, he argued, must "restore sanity and reason" by clearing Paxton.

According to a document from the committee, the House procedure will begin with opening remarks on Saturday and go through four hours of discussion, closing remarks, and a vote.

Paxton, who spent five terms in the house before being elected a state senator, is now facing dismal math.

Although it is unknown how many allies he may have in the House, an impeachment just requires a simple majority. That indicates that if all 64 Democrats vote against Paxton, just a tiny portion of the 85 Republican lawmakers would also need to do so. Paxton's wife, Senator Angela, is a member of the Senate, where a two-thirds majority is needed for final expulsion.

With the campaign to impeach Paxton, one of the GOP's most renowned legal defenders, who in 2020 requested the U.S. Supreme Court to reverse President Joe Biden's triumph, might see an unexpectedly swift demise.

For years, the FBI has been looking into allegations that Paxton exploited his position to assist a contributor. He hasn't been tried despite being separately charged with securities fraud in 2015.

Tuesday, when the findings of the five-member committee's probe were made public, Paxton claimed Phelan had launched a political assault, accusing the speaker of being intoxicated on the House floor and demanding his resignation. This was dismissed by Phelan's office as an effort to "save face."

Just seven months after handily securing a third term, Paxton faces impeachment. George P. Bush was one of his rivals who encouraged voters to remove the tainted incumbent from office but found that many either were unaware of Paxton's long list of alleged wrongdoings or thought they were just political charges.

According to state legislation, the House is still able to embark on the impeachment process even if the regular session is about to conclude on Monday. The two chambers might reconvene at a later time.

Paxton's connection with one of his affluent contributors, his alleged efforts to shield the donor from an FBI investigation, and his attempts to obstruct whistleblower concerns made by his staff are the main causes of the articles of impeachment.

In a certain way, Paxton's political predicament came about quickly: the committee inquiry broke on Tuesday, and the following day, an unusual public exposure of his alleged illegal behavior followed.

However, the criticism of Paxton was long in coming, according to his critics.

He acknowledged breaking Texas securities law in 2014 by recruiting customers without being registered as an investment adviser. Paxton was accused of scamming investors in a software business and was charged with felony securities charges by a grand jury in his hometown close to Dallas a year later. He has entered a not-guilty plea to two felony offenses that may result in a five to 99-year jail term.

Opening a legal defense fund, he took $100,000 from a businessman whose organization was being looked into by Paxton's office for Medicaid fraud. A retired Arizonan who had a son named Paxton who was subsequently employed for a high-ranking position but promptly sacked for exhibiting child pornography in a meeting gave an extra $50,000 to the cause.

His association with rich benefactor and Austin businessman Nate Paul has exposed Paxton to the greatest danger.

Many Paxton's senior aides expressed concerns to the FBI in 2020 about the attorney general abused his authority to support Paul over unsubstantiated accusations that a complex plot to steal $200 million worth of his properties was afoot. Paul's house was raided by the FBI in 2019, but he hasn't been prosecuted and his lawyers have said he did nothing illegal. Paxton also admitted to having an affair with a lady who subsequently turned out to be Paul's employee.

The impeachment allegations include claims that Paxton inappropriately provided legal advice to Paul's advantage, attempted to tamper with foreclosure litigation, and fired, harassed, and interfered with personnel who alerted management to what was happening. The allegations of bribery originate from Paul reportedly hiring the subject of Paxton's romance in return for legal assistance and Paul allegedly footing the bill for lavish upgrades to Paxton's Austin home.

The repairs on the house, which was also under FBI investigation, were not paid for by Paul, according to a senior attorney for Paxton's office on Friday. Chris Hilton's comment during the press conference, one of the few direct comments from Paxton's team to the impeachment articles, that "He paid for all his home repairs and renovations," was one of the few.

Other counts, such as lying to state investigators, stem from Paxton's ongoing 2015 felony securities fraud indictment.

The eight assistants who informed the FBI about Paxton were all terminated or resigned, and four eventually filed lawsuits under Texas' whistleblower statute. Paxton made a $3.3 million settlement offer in February, which the House must now approve.

The investigation committee said on Friday that Paxton's demand for compensation was what sparked their inquiry.

We cannot stress enough that Paxton would not be facing impeachment by the House if it weren't for his desire for a taxpayer-funded settlement for his improper behavior, the panel added.

Chapter 3: Donald Trump Jr., Conservative Republicans Ride to Ken Paxton's Defense On Eve of Impeachment Vote

On the eve of the impeachment vote, Ken Paxton is defended by conservative Republicans including Donald Trump Jr.

The attorney general's defenders characterize the impeachment vote on Saturday as a political witch hunt designed to eliminate President Joe Biden's greatest burden.

Following a Texas House committee's recommendation to impeach Attorney General Ken Paxton on Thursday, numerous well-known Republicans on Friday adopted a similar tactic: attack, attack, attack.

Conservatives said that their fellow Republicans in the Texas House, including Speaker Dade Phelan, were trying to discredit conservatives and voters by assaulting Paxton in remarks and social media postings. And they painted Paxton as the target of a political witch hunt that was organized by a group of Democrats and "Republicans in name only," mostly without addressing the substance of the many claims made against him.

According to Matt Rinaldi, head of the Texas Republican Party, "the impeachment proceedings against the Attorney General are but the latest front in the Texas House's war against Republicans to stop the conservative direction of our state." "The Phelan leadership team empowered Democrats, allowed them to hold leadership positions, and allowed them to control the agenda, which resulted in this sham impeachment."

Republican from Texas in the highest position to criticize the probe thus far is Rinaldi. Lt. Gov. Dan Patrick, who would preside over an impeachment trial in the Senate, has said it would be inappropriate for Gov. Greg Abbott to comment. Gov. Greg Abbott has kept mute.

But national Republicans are stepping forward to fill the gap. While former president Donald Trump, a supporter of Paxton who gave his campaign a boost before the GOP primary last year, has been silent, his son Donald Trump Jr. called the probe against "America First patriot Ken Paxton" on Friday a "disgrace."

"MAGA opposes this RINO/DEMO led witch hunt!" said Ken Paxton. Tweets from Trump Jr.

Paxton has received support from other well-known right-wing personalities in a similar manner. Former Trump advisor Stephen Miller urged conservatives to "stand with Ken" in light of Paxton's many legal actions against the Biden administration. Kyle Rittenhouse, who shot two Black Lives Matter protestors in Wisconsin to death but was cleared of murder charges, charged Phelan with working with "anti-gun Democrats" and "attacking our pro-gun attorney general."

The assaults on Phelan are not brand-new: Phelan has been the target of months of criticism from extreme right Republicans who claim he is holding up passage of conservative legislation in the House, which has historically been more moderate than the Senate.

A clear indicator of the high-stakes drama that has gripped the state since Tuesday, when Paxton accused Phelan of presiding over the House while intoxicated and demanded his resignation, is the fact that this week's charges have been exceptionally nasty and personal.

The results of a two-month inquiry into years of alleged misbehavior and legal violations by the attorney general were made public the next day by the House General Investigating Committee.

The committee, which consisted of three Republicans and two Democrats, met briefly on Thursday afternoon and unanimously decided to forward articles of impeachment to the whole House. After the pandemonium of the previous days had subsided on Friday, Paxton and his allies launched an offensive in anticipation of a discussion and vote on the issue in the House on Saturday afternoon.

In a short statement on Friday, Paxton accused the Republican-led Texas House of attempting to undermine him and his tenacious legal challenges against President Joe Biden's policies. Paxton specifically addressed Biden at least eight times in the speech, and he condemned the impeachment process as unfair and unethical.

This week, similar assertions have been made by several well-known Republicans.

Right-wing Texas Scorecard editor Michael Quinn Sullivan said, "Get one thing clear: The impeachment of Ken Paxton by the

Texas House is motivated by the crony elite that wants to get along with the Biden administration.

Sullivan's organization is closely connected to a group of West Texas oil tycoons, including Tim Dunn and the Wilks brothers, who have given Paxton modest sums.

Campaign finance reports revealed that Dunn and the Wilks have contributed at least $1.4 million in individual donations and another $870,000 via their numerous fundraising organizations, including Defend Texas Liberty PAC, making them among Paxton's most prolific contributors since 2002.

Last year, Defend Texas Liberty unsuccessfully attempted to replace Abbott and Phelan with more conservative candidates by spending more than $5 million. Candidates endorsed by the party have been by far the most outspoken opponents of Phelan this session, notably Bryan Slaton, the former Royse City lawmaker who was expelled from the House this year for having sex with a juvenile staffer after offering her alcohol.

Defend Texas Liberty urged supporters to call their lawmakers on Friday and express their disapproval of the inquiry in a series of bulk text texts. One text message said, "Don't let them work with Democrats to steal your vote."

A few Paxton supporters were there in the gallery seats above the House floor on Friday as the assaults against Phelan went on. One local GOP leader claimed to have driven two hours to stand up for Paxton because she feels the Democratic establishment and Phelan are trying to discredit him.

According to Bulverde Spring Branch Conservative Republicans president Kaci Sisk, Paxton is the most successful attorney general this state has ever had. "Those who support impeachment are essentially supporting the Biden administration and the state's dishonest district attorneys. We don't mind that he was charged. We could care less.

Others who support Sisk have mirrored his lack of interest in Paxton's 2015 charges on two counts of felony securities fraud and discounted the House committee's inquiry as a tired old story.

Two years after high-level subordinates in the attorney general's office accused Paxton of taking bribes and other crimes, Paxton was reelected in 2018 and again in 2022 despite the charges.

Supporters of the candidate claim the probe is a hoax designed to suppress voter will by bringing up well-known scandals as justification for impeachment, citing those wins.

Rep. Steve Toth, R-The Woodlands, stated his opposition to impeachment on Thursday, claiming that it would be "illegal" to do so if it included actions that occurred before Paxton's most recent election.

House investigators disputed such assertions.

The General Investigating Committee emphasized in a memo to lawmakers that Paxton's request earlier this year for the Legislature to pay $3.3 million to settle a whistleblower lawsuit brought by four agency executives who were fired after raising concerns about Paxton's actions to law enforcement served as the impetus for the committee's investigation.

The document also addressed claims made by attorneys for the attorney general's office that the committee probe was unlawful since Paxton could not be impeached for offenses allegedly committed before his 2022 reelection. According to the document, Paxton's situation did not fall within the so-called "forgiveness doctrine."

The committee said that four articles connected to Governor James Ferguson's behavior before and after the 1916 election led to his impeachment in 1917. Ferguson was removed from office when the Senate found him guilty on the charges.

Chapter 4: What Allegations Led to the House Investigation?

Senior members of Mr. Paxton's team requested a probe of their boss's conduct in a letter they sent in 2020. The aides said that Mr. Paxton exploited his position to further Nate Paul's interests, a political contributor and friend of the attorney general.

After being subjected to a federal agent raid at his home and place of business in 2019, Mr. Paul, a rich Austin real estate owner, got in touch with Mr. Paxton. In defiance of his staff's strident protests, Mr. Paxton took the extraordinary step of approving a state probe of the F.B.I.'s operations. Although he had no prior expertise as a prosecutor, investigators for the House committee claimed he selected an outside attorney who identified himself as a special prosecutor to handle it. The F.B.I. has not made any comments on its inquiry.

Mr. Paxton said in a statement at the time that he had "never been driven by a desire to protect a political donor or to abuse this office, and I never will."

In a letter dated 2020, Mr. Paxton's aides claimed that he had engaged in bribery, misuse of authority, and other "potential criminal offenses." Four of the assistants also voiced their concerns to the Texas Rangers and F.B.I.

The four assistants also expressed their worries to the attorney general's office, according to court documents in the case; a few weeks later, they were all sacked. After that, the assistants claimed Mr. Paxton had retaliated against them in a lawsuit.

The investigation continued, and Mr. Paxton's office eventually issued a 374-page report that said, "A.G. Paxton committed no crime." He has also filed an appeal, but a Texas court of appeals has rejected his arguments. In a deal with the four former top staffers, Mr. Paxton agreed to pay $3.3 million in February.

How did it result in the potential for impeachment?

The 2020 claims have been the subject of further scrutiny due to concerns regarding how to pay the payment.

Mr. Paxton requested money from the Texas Legislature to pay the $3.3 million. That use of public funds was opposed by Republican House Speaker Dade Phelan, a conventional conservative. According to the spokesperson for Mr. Phelan, the House has opened an inquiry into the accusations to learn more about the funding request.

The accusations stated in the aides' complaint meant that many of the investigators' conclusions on Mr. Paxton were already known to the general public.

But on Thursday, a House committee vote delivered the first formal verdict on those accusations: Lawmakers determined they were sufficient to start the process of ousting Mr. Paxton from office.

What exactly are the articles of impeachment?
The committee on Thursday submitted 20 articles of impeachment against Mr. Paxton. The Republican head of the committee, Andrew Murr, said that they detailed "grave offenses" as they were being distributed across the House chamber.

The articles accuse Mr. Paxton of a long list of wrongdoings, including accepting bribes, failing to uphold his official duties, hindering the legal system in a separate securities fraud case that is pending against him, making false representations on official papers and reports, and abusing the public's confidence.

Many of the allegations, according to the committee, were the numerous ways Mr. Paxton had allegedly exploited his position to Mr. Paul's advantage and fired people in the office who objected to his behavior.

Additionally, Mr. Paxton is charged with profiting "from Nate Paul's employment of a woman with whom Paxton was having an extramarital affair" and interfering in a lawsuit brought by the Roy F. and Joann Cole Mitte Foundation, an Austin-based nonprofit organization, against Mr. Paul's businesses.

What more legal difficulties does Mr. Paxton face?

The staffers' concerns about corruption and retribution led to the opening of a federal inquiry, but no charges have yet been brought as a consequence.

However, Mr. Paxton has been charged with a crime throughout the majority of his time serving as the state's attorney general.

Mr. Paxton was arrested and lodged in a county prison outside of Dallas in 2015—his first year in that position—after being charged with a felony for securities fraud. In the years before he was appointed attorney general, Mr. Paxton allegedly worked in the securities industry and deceived customers and investors by, among other things, omitting to disclose to them that he would get a commission on their investment.

The matter has not yet gone to trial, and he has denied any wrongdoing.

Articles of impeachment released this week charged the attorney general with obstructing justice in that case, asserting that a lawsuit brought by a supporter of Mr. Paxton's campaign effectively postponed the trial.

What comes after that?
On Saturday at 1pm, the House will vote on the impeachment measure, according to the head of the committee looking into Mr. Paxton.

If Mr. Paxton were to be impeached, he would be temporarily removed from office while awaiting a trial on the accusations in the State Senate, where some of his closest friends, including his wife, would serve as jurors. The Senate's business might be postponed until beyond Monday's conclusion of the ordinary parliamentary session. The time of the Senate's next meeting and the trial's scheduling are both quite unknown.

According to Christopher Hilton, a lawyer for Mr. Paxton, the committee's procedure for drafting the articles of impeachment was "completely lacking," and the points cited had already been thoroughly discussed during Mr. Paxton's successful re-election campaign last year.

Mr. Hilton further claimed that Texas law only permitted impeachment for actions that occurred after the previous election, giving rise to speculation that the proceedings would face a judicial challenge. In the articles of impeachment, the majority of the charges relate to behavior that took place earlier.